Paleo For Beginners

A 14-Day Paleo Diet Plan For A Simple Start To The Paleo Diet

Marc Morris

Table of Contents

Introduction to Paleo's origins

As a modern day, nutritional diet, Paleo is appropriately referred as the caveman's diet, the Stone Age diet, or even the hunter-gatherer's diet among popular nutritional circuits; using these terms makes the origins of this diet more or less transparent and easier to view the evolutionary changes in our diet and lifestyle as a chart, mapping the changes in our overall health, over the centuries. The Paleolithic era prevailed for a period of 2.5 million and ended with the domestication of animals and some major agricultural revolution and although, we're at the forefront of technology and scientific advancements today, our modernity and increased knowledge of how our body works, hasn't managed to scale down the epidemic of common health ailments that have been escalating mortality rates and reducing life spans all over the globe on a daily basis.

My digression to current health stats, worldwide, isn't intended to take anything away from Paleo's rich history. But it clearly speaks volumes for the transparency of the diet's overall effect on our human bodies, something credibility noticeable, if you compare our diet now and the mind boggling recent health statistics. About 10,000 years ago, men and women were used to a living with a vastly different diet and lifestyle, which affected their health and life spans positively. They were used to excitable food patterns, which required them to hunt, chase, and spear their food, and avoid fatal personal injury in the process. But this just scratches the surface of their seemingly simple lifestyle. Cavemen were nomads; they weren't used to the comfort of a permanent residence like most of us today.

It's easy to gauge that modern conveniences are something Paleolithic men and women were in dire need of, but whether all of these conveniences have in retrospect improved our circumstances, remains to be seen. This book will talk about Paleo and its ability to give us infinite health within its prescribed parameters. You will immediately find yourself thinking about other fad diets and comparing, or applying their potential of failure to the Paleo diet. The one thing I can promise you is that Paleo is not a fad diet. It's a diet which has shaped our body chemistry to what it is today and eating and living a different lifestyle has forced our bodies to respond negatively by compromising our immune systems and general health and wellbeing.

From personal experience, I'm one of the unlucky millions who suffer from some form of gluten intolerance (we'll cover the specifics of what gluten intolerance is all about in the coming chapters of the book). Like many others, I've always been a firm believer of a balanced diet and have followed USDA's approved food pyramid year after year, but I've found myself increasingly uncomfortable in my overall health and wellbeing following my 30th birthday. It's uncanny how some health issues, which have only been a mild nuisance in our younger years can start escalating with a vengeance once you hit that milestone in your age. Not that 30 is some precursor to old age, but some bodily functions can change around that time, signaling an inevitable slide into the first of our natural ageing process. The first signs of wrinkles creep up in those areas you've probably never even acknowledged before. Your metabolism slows down a few notches, and those pounds you incidentally piled on after thanksgiving or Christmas holidays become even harder to slough off than they used to be. All these are just general ageing symptoms without adding lifestyle to the equation (married? single? with kids? A whole new ball game). Truth? no one wants to feel the effects of 'ageing' any sooner than they have to, but there are many people who manage to avoid these 'effects' by keeping their diets clean and nutritious. No myth, just the truth, if you get a good amount of fresh air, keep a balanced diet, which doesn't end up causing diabetes, hypertension, obesity, etc. then you're likely to keep yourself younger than most people your age.

Scientifically, diet and lifestyle have always had the ability to slow down aging and general wear and tear of the years. Several health journals and magazines can tell us that our current diet is chock full of dangerous additives, preservatives and artificial nutrition, which adds nothing to your health. Instead of seeking nutritious substitutes we've gotten used to eating more commercially produced foods full of sugar and refined carbohydrates. If you feel like you've had just about enough of health anarchy lately, let the 14 day Paleo diet plan give you something better to look forward to!

So, what will you get from this book?

- History of the Paleo diet and lifestyle.
- A low down of what the Paleo lifestyle is all about and where you should start from.
- The basics of Paleo and macronutrient ratio, which should help you figure out what you're Paleo requirements are.
- A list of foods that are Paleo approved and those which aren't approved by Paleo.
- A look at why gluten is on the permanently banned list of Paleo foods.
- A 14 day meal plan to help you get started on your Paleo journey.
- 14 nutritious Breakfasts, lunches, dinners, snacks and desserts, which will make you're transitioning to Paleo easier.
- Several tips and recommendations to make it easier for Paleo beginners.

Chapter 1

Paleo cleanse anyone? – Paleo diet and lifestyle basics

If you're not new to the Paleo circuit, by now, you must know that Paleo is not a fad diet which was introduced as a simplified concoction to give you temporary relief from weight problems, autoimmune disorders, or other varying ailments for which diets have been developed to lend a temporary hand in healing. Paleo, or the primal lifestyle as it's called in various nutritional circles was known to exist around 12,000 ago. This was a lifestyle, which was inadvertently followed by the regular caveman of Stone Ages. This diet was and lifestyle was considerably limited in its applications before any advancements. This is not to say that scientific discoveries and technological advances are something that should or could have been avoided. After all, over the centuries, our quest for improving lifestyle and diet have brought us this far. We no longer need to hunt for our food, or chase it. The agricultural revolution even helped us feed the world's growing population and avoid food shortages. And being as man is a creature of curiosity and adaptation, our mindsets have adapted to all the changes around us remarkably well. And yet, somehow, the same can't be said about our changing diets or the significant increase in human mortality rates and autoimmune diseases. Considering all the recent strides in medicine, we still haven't found cures for major degenerative diseases like cancers, diabetes, Alzheimer's and heart diseases. Modern medical science can't seem to provide a sound concoction in the form of pill that can fully cure these problems. Relying on diet and lifestyle, however, can help reduce your risk of developing any of these major health problems and improve our well being tremendously.

Paleolithic men and women relied on simple Paleolithic objectives, which shaped their body chemistry and gave them their optimum health levels. How can we be sure of their optimal health stats? Several scientific studies conducted over the years show that Stone Age man rarely ever suffered from the many modern medical diseases that have become increasingly common. Heart diseases, diabetes, and cancer were one of the major degenerative diseases, which never existed in the times of cavemen. In those days, your life span shortened for one of two reasons, if you were fatally wounded by a wild beast you were chasing for food or from infectious diseases that set in from untreated fatal wounds (antibiotics and penicillin had a long way to be discovered). You may think that the older topographic conditions and food availability played an important role in giving them their healthy bodies, but really, a combination of factors played a role in ensuring that they survived harsh winters and wild animal ambushes.

Food: The cavemen were used to consuming a wide variety of animal meat, birds, fish, nuts, seeds, and plants even as far back as 12,000 ago. Due to their hunter-gatherer dynamic, their diet was hugely varied because none of the animals that existed at those times can be found now; large woolly mammals, large flightless birds, and giant hornless rhinos were normally hunted by the cavemen; they generally settled camps near the coasts in order to supplement their diets with fresh fish, seaweed, and shellfish. There were only a few ways to store food for longer periods, which didn't involve any artificial preservatives. So, food had to be consumed quickly. The women were generally entrusted the task of gathering fruits and plants, while men hunted the animals. When they had exhausted the available resources, or when food was no longer available in that particular area, they would just move on from there and find another settlement which had abundant resources. Later on, when these nomadic tribes discovered agriculture, they found that it permitted them to start settlements and quit the nomadic patterns they were so used to because they could cultivate their own food and feed their tribes without having to exhaust resources of a particular land.

Skills: Even hunting and gathering food required a wide range of skills. You had to know how to throw a spear, chase or corner a large animal before it could mortally wound the hunter. Cavemen were very knowledgeable about their general environment, poisonous plants to avoid or medicinal properties for various other plant species, and animal behavior, which helped them with tracking and hunting their food. The hunters were adept at bringing down large beasts, finding safe places to take shelter temporarily, or looking for plants with great medicinal properties. Their situational awareness was at an all time high. Something most of us struggle with, in our daily lives. Most of us wouldn't know what to take other then paracetamol when we come down with the flu, or when our joints ache. The prehistoric man did not need meteorologists of whether reports to tell them bad weather was approaching, they're observation skills were off the chart. They maintained focus levels and general alertness with sleep cycles that differ from our general 7-8 hour sleep schedule. Sleep is important to our health as it is to mental prowess, but as opposed to an uninterrupted cycle of 7-8 hours, the cavemen sometimes relied on shifts or short naps throughout the day to fulfill their requirement of sleep. This worked out well to ensure that while some of the group slept safely, others remained on guard, able to alert others when a in case of a predatory attack.

Lifestyle: When we think of lifestyle now, we think of occasional exercise at the gym, or some quick cardio. We count on our cars to get us wherever we need to go, even if the destination might be two streets away. The concept of natural muscle movement has all but ceased to exist. This brings us to the caveman lifestyle, which differed in every possible way from our modern existence; the average caveman got a lot of exercise in their daily life without really aiming to burn a certain amount of calories, their diets were high energy diets and their ingredients were pure and untreated by any chemicals. This meant they had high energy levels to burn. The food they ate, gave them enough strength to chase after daily necessities to survive. They climbed, dragged, pushed, pulled, lunged, sprinted, etc. enough in their daily routine to develop stronger muscles and had impressive endurance levels due to regular low intensity cardio like walking for long periods of times at a slower pace. They sprinted after food and threw spears with enough force to strengthen and build muscles. This was natural muscle movement for them, which gave them leaner bodies without aiming for higher muscle masses and higher endurance levels. Their natural activity levels endorsed their exercise quota.

Looking at these three factors you can tell there's a lot more to Paleo then just a being a diet which promotes high energy levels. It's the complete lifestyle, which promotes positive wellbeing and overall health as opposed to just eating certain kinds of foods. Diet and lifestyle worked in conjunction for the caveman to get them through rough weather, bad terrains, and difficult living conditions. These are the qualities have helped shape our body's chemistry for what it is today. Our bodies have adapted to a myriad of changes around the world in the last 10,000 years, except for our current living and eating habits. If you look at the health statistics and compare them to the increasingly artificial enhancements to our foods and living habits, you can see where changes can help improve these numbers.

Some recent health statistics given by the CDC (Centre for disease control and prevention), The National cancer institute, and celiac central.org show how the most common diseases have escalated to an all-time high:

- About 1 in 4 deaths occur due to heart disease in America (that's a whopping 600,000 deaths a year!).

- Coronary heart disease is ranked as the most common heart disease, which annually kills about 380,000 people.

- 720,000 American people die annually of heart attacks. Out of this number, about 60% that die had a heart attack for the first time, the remaining number indicates people who died of a second heart attack.

- According to the American health association, most problems like high blood pressure, diabetes, smoking, inactivity, bad food habits, and obesity are all linked to risk of developing heart diseases.

- By 2010 there were about 1.9 million cases of diabetes 2 recorded among Americans ages 20 and above.

- The current statistics show that 25.6 million Americans suffer from diabetes 2 who are older than 20.

- An estimated 83% of celiac disease cases remain undiagnosed.

- At least 1 in 133 people in America suffer from celiac disease.

- Around 22% of people suffering from celiac disease have an immediate family member who also has celiac disease.

- The current worldwide mortality rate due to cancer is at least 8,201,030 deaths a year.

The purpose of these statistics isn't purely for shock and horror. It's to show how modern influences and lifestyle changes have drastically compromised mortality rates and general disease statistics, which were always considered confined to a certain age, sex, or region.

Even the most common of diseases these days, like heart disease was first detected only about 3,500 years ago, found in Egyptian mummies. Pharaoh Merenptah died in 1203 BC, from atherosclerosis, which is the narrowing of arteries. Out of 16 of the mummies studied for heart disease, 9 had confirmed cases of the same heart disease. This at the very least tells you that you diet and lifestyle patterns, while dramatically changed for the better in some ways, (i.e. we learnt how to preserve food better, developed ways to mature crops quicker and increase yield to feed the masses), it however, made us more unassuming of our diets nutritional value over the years.

a. **How does the Paleolithic diet differ from the USDA's recommended diet?**

Paleo is a diet and lifestyle of simpler times, but not in the way you might think; the cavemen were not privy to our way to sautéing and pan frying meat in those days. Their methods of cooking and handling ingredients were much simpler and based more upon a means to an end because their daily activity levels demanded equally nutritious sustenance. They had different ingredients from what we're used to today, but the end result was the same. So, let's get to know what eating Paleo is all about and how it will enrich your diet and lifestyle.

1. Paleo as a diet is about eating animal meat, fish, and poultry which is of the grass fed variety and not grain fed because nutritional levels in grain fed meat is far less as compared to the grass fed variety. For example, Grass fed cow meat contains 4 times more omega 3 as compared to the grain fed cow meat, which is readily available.

2. Fruits and vegetables are considered a great source of fiber and rich with vitamins and nutrients which boost your energy levels and keep you healthy. There are exceptions like roots and tubers which are starchy, or have a high glycemic index levels (G.I. index levels indicate how quickly a food increases blood sugar levels.) The Paleo diet considers fruits and vegetables with lower glycemic index levels healthy and highly nutritious as sides or snacks with your main meals.

3. Fats and oils in Paleo are healthier and consist of nut oils like coconut oil, olive oil, avocado oil, coconut oil, etc. as compared to any seed oils, which are high in bad saturated fats, an accumulation of which can be harmful to your hearts health. Paleo also uses natural occurring fats like ghee, and grass fed sources of butter as well because they are pure and not chemically altered or enhanced like trans fats

(used in commercially produced foods like crisps, cookies, doughnuts, cakes, etc.).

4. Many Paleo followers tend to stay away from dairy because they're lactose intolerant and strict Paleo advocates have always made out dairy to be irrelevant to our diets because large animal domestication only took place a few thousand years ago and their domestication timelines varied according to the types of animals that existed at a time in different regions. Fact based Paleo considers dairy products one of those grey areas in the diet, which is open to debate and assumption. If you're lactose intolerant and aren't sure about the effects of dairy on your body, try cutting it out of your diet along with the other ingredients which aren't Paleo approved and see the different by adding it back slowly. If dairy doesn't suit you and you still want to include it in recipes, etc. try nondairy versions like coconut milk, almond milk, etc. This way you can still make those delicious desserts you crave without the guilt of it damaging your health.

5. Cereal grains are the most popular form of food all over the world. Recent world consumption levels show that it's the fastest growing food over the last few decades and is at an all-time high production level. Cavemen were not used to consuming cereal grains and the later agricultural revolutions brought grains which were originally very different from

the grains consumed today. Today, our grains have been genetically modified beyond a recognizable level and host a toxic protein called gluten, which affects our body negatively by attacking our immune systems and diminishing our capability of consuming nutrients that come from foods. The health statistics on gluten allergies or celiac disease (as it's called now) shows a rapid increase its incidence and that the human body is clearly not suited to consume cereal grains. When you're on the Paleo diet, consider cereal grains public enemy number 1 and avoid it like the plague!

6. Refined carbohydrates and sugar laced food has become the norm today. Cavemen were used to some primitive form of sugar in the form of raw honey and fruits. They were healthy and lean because they didn't pack on pounds with foods that have empty calories. There are several conclusive studies which show that overconsumption of sugar and refined carbohydrates are linked to heart disease, obesity, chronic acne, and even cancer. Paleo recommends cutting out all sugar and foods that have refined carbohydrates. Sodium content in processed foods is also of some concern these days because high sodium consumption levels overtime can lead to blood pressure problems.

7. Legumes and lentils have gotten a bad rap from Paleo experts because of toxins like phytates and

lectins, which limit your nutrient consumption and damage the lining of your small intestines, letting unwanted substances leak into your blood stream. However, you can reduce the phytate and lectin content in legumes drastically by soaking them for a while before cooking them. So, this is another grey area ingredient in Paleo that most Paleo experts are on the fence about.

b. Paleo myths debunked – Why should you follow the Paleo diet

Like all other health improvement diets that get the 'fad' treatment, Paleo is measured against various perceived notions and reservations many of us have when we're asked to part with our favorite foods and beverages to reach that elusive goal of good health many of are decidedly lacking these days. It's normal to be skeptical of something you haven't given much thought to before, or aren't well informed about; Paleo as a diet and lifestyle choice can be hard to get behind for several simpler reasons as opposed to it being a problematic diet, which is based on idealistic expectations of a good outcome. Some of these questions might answer your curiosity and soothe your skeptic nerves about Paleo's positive intentions.

1. **How can we be expected to follow a diet followed by cavemen who lived 12,000 years ago? This just doesn't add up.**

This is something many of us may start wondering about when we consider Paleo's origins. The average caveman did live 12,000 years ago and he consumed a variety of meat, fish, seeds, and plants, which aren't even available now, or have evolved into different organisms, only distantly related in their nutritional attributes. But, from all this we can at least surmise that the caveman ate nutritiously unpolluted forms of food that doesn't even vaguely resemble what we eat today. They lived healthier lives, which based on conclusive studies into Paleolithic remains were cut short only by things like infections because there were no concoctions similar to antibiotics at those times; brutal animal attacks hunters couldn't fend off, or most of the time, death due to harsh weather conditions. Today's list of fatalistic diseases caused by what we eat overtime isn't as short or easily explainable, not to mention, our activity levels today aren't what they used to be at all. We no longer rely on our legs as much as we used to as we have machines to get us where we need to go, there isn't a lot of running and sprinting needed, unless we're fitness buffs, athletes, or training for the Olympics. The concept of natural muscle movement has become all but obsolete and irrelevant. Now we're just lazy, disinterested, and reliant on quick methods of diet satiation (all of which involve processed junk). All nutritional circles and physicians, whether they favor the Paleo diet, the DASH diet, or the Mediterranean diet agree on one thing, there is nothing wrong with eating a healthy and balanced diet. Consider this, a balanced diet has the right amount of Protein, Fats and Carbohydrates; this means that any food which fulfills the appropriate macronutrient ratio levels and isn't full of harmful preservatives, additives, or pesticide, should be okay to consume in the long term diet.

2. Paleo is considered a high protein diet. Isn't too much protein dangerous for our health?

Eating and living Paleo is all about living healthy, not about losing awareness of real health issues whether they are caused by eating our current diet or reverting to the Paleo diet. Eating more Protein has been raised as one of those serious concerns, which can deter readers from thinking or changing over to this diet. But Paleo is nothing if not balanced and reliable as a healthy diet and lifestyle that restores vibrancy your body may have lost over the years. Eating the right kind of Protein in the right amount is the key to carry on your vitality and not lose it because of toxins accumulating due to overconsumption of protein. This is something that isn't exclusive to Paleo even though as a diet, it encourages eating more Proteins. There is a limit to what amount of protein is suitable for each person, depending on their age, gender, and activity levels.

Having less than 10% of Protein in your daily diet can also be problematic for health, but since the Paleo diet is always more of a high Protein and low carbohydrate diet, most won't have an issue with the effects of low Protein levels in their diets. A 20-29% Protein ratio is considered high, but not necessarily an issue if you pair it with the right amount of Carbohydrates and Fats. Protein toxicity (the result of consuming an excess of proteins) can occur if you're not careful about pairing your Protein content with the appropriate Fat and Carbohydrate content to balance it because they help your body in processing Protein's. When your body breaks down Proteins into energy, the kidneys first need to remove the nitrate content from the resulting amino acids by a process known as deanimation. A by-product called ammonia emerges, which is pretty toxic. The liver then sets to change the ammonia into a waste product called urea, which can then pass through your urine as waste. But if you eat too much protein you will be putting too much stress on your kidneys and liver. Eating more Proteins without accompanying Fats and Carbohydrates will not only overwork your liver and kidneys, but you will also not get enough of fat soluble micronutrients that are essential for your other bodily functions.

So, the lesson to learn from this is that Paleo is a high protein diet because it uses proteins as energy compared to the usual carbohydrates, but how much protein is too high for you? Consider your age, your sex, and you're activity levels because the recommended levels of proteins in the Paleo diet vary for different age groups, sexes, and for those of us who have low activity levels, moderate, or higher activity levels. We'll talk about the appropriate, recommended macronutrient levels for different groups of people in the next section.

3. Paleo as a diet, sounds like it can be really restrictive.

Many of us read into this diet as some restrictive challenge or a battle of nerves to see how long we can hold out on certain foods. Paleo isn't a restrictive diet; it has elements, which are restrictive for legitimate reasons, other than to just spite our evolved eating habits. Grains are actually the hybridized version of what they used to be decades ago or even centuries ago. We no longer consume the same nutrients or benefits because of the gluten content present in them. Those who find cutting out grains impossibly restrictive, understandably feel themselves having a culinary crises because many of our recipes-savory and sweet use the grains and grain by-products. Gluten is now even found in certain our common condiments and tea.

For those who are allergic to gluten and attribute poor health to it, need no further provocation to cut all grains out of their lives, but those of us who either have mild undertones of symptoms that may or may not be gluten allergy related, tend to stick to eating grains in one form or the other. So, what is gluten? It's a protein, which nourishes the seed, while it grows. In the late 1950's farmers discovered that if they harvested the crop before it fully matured the gluten content in them would be far greater and this larger gluten content was responsible for great results in baking. Dough's tend to raise more with higher gluten content, and is pretty much responsible for the texture in food products, i.e. elasticity and fluffiness of breads.

The problem is, with celiac disease, not all together easily diagnosed in many people as compared to those with severe cases of gluten allergies, many of us may not know we suffer from gluten allergies or celiac disease. The symptoms are varied and can differ according to your age, sex, grain consumption levels.

A list of symptoms that have been attributed to eating grains:

- Muscle cramps and joint pains

- Digestive problems accompanied by diarrhea, bloating, abdominal pain, gas, and weight loss.

- Skin rashes

- Mouth ulcers

- Missed menstrual periods for women

- Growth problems in children

- Iron deficiency (anemia)

- Birth defects due to poor absorption of nutrients like folic acid

- Miscarriages and infertility

- Osteoporosis because the body can't absorb enough calcium and Vitamin D.

- Intestinal cancer (rare)

- A combination of the above problems or some of them can lead to other diseases make you more susceptible to thyroid disease, Type 1 diabetes, arthritis, lupus, gout, etc.

And these are only issues attributed to the consumption of grains over time. Legumes, while, they aren't as invasive as gluten can be equally harmful, if they aren't soaked for a lengthy period of time before being cooked. An earlier paragraph talks about the lectins and phytates in legumes and how they can be damaging to our health. However, if you can reduce the lectin and phytate levels significantly through soaking them and if you're body generally responds well to them, they can be treated as a grey area food in the Paleo diet, and be included once in a while in your diet. Not only are legumes a cheaper source of protein, there are many people who aren't avid meat eaters, would like a change every now and then, or are straight out vegetarians. If you soak them for a good period of time the anti-nutrients in them don't interfere with your absorption of vital nutrients. Plus, pairing them with vegetables or seafood can make for a great combination as well as a cheaper meal in daily routine as compared to expensive cuts of lean, grass fed meat.

On a whole, Paleo's purpose is to give you long term health benefits, not brief flashes of them. Having restrictive elements like avoidance of sugary foods, and refined carbohydrates, trans fats, and over consumption of high Carbohydrate foods help with flushing out toxins from your body and protects it from artificial additives and preservatives, which have been recorded as being detrimental to our health at any given time. So, you decide whether the restrictive elements work or it's just too restrictive to work for you.

c. Macronutrient ratios - How does the division affect your body?

We discussed the importance of a balanced diet, based on the right macronutrient ratio for you. This ratio will help you determine the portion sizes of Fats, carbohydrates and Protein which should be in your daily routine. All three macronutrients are important to the health equation and they cooperate together to give your body strength and vitality. Let's start by discussing their roles in your body and what makes them so important. Once you know how they interact with your body's chemistry you'll be able to decide on the right ratio for you.

Fats

Fats have always been treated as a nutritional pariah in our notion of balanced diets. We've been repeatedly told Fat free and low fat is the way to stay healthy and the more Fats you cut out, the better you'll feel and the lesser heart disease cases will come up in next world health statistics. While, overconsumption of any macronutrient on its own can be dangerous and harmful to your body, a moderate level of Fat can actually elevate your health and help balance your diet as well. Even USDA's published report on dietary intakes shows that about 20% to 35% of our calories should come from Fats. Considering, Fats are actually the most concentrated source of energy and help your body in absorbing certain nutrients like A, D, E, K and Beta carotene, they probably deserve a little more praise than they actually receive. Even more importantly, Fat's help in maintaining our cell membranes and give our internal organs cushioning. It's really the type of Fat you consume that should be of some concern. There are three types of Fat's that are commonly consumed in today's society; saturated fats, unsaturated fats, and trans fats. Saturated fats come from butter, lard, cream, cheese, etc. and trans fats come from processed foods and snacks. As a diet, Paleo encourages us to use more of unsaturated fats like olive oil, avocado oil, and canola oil and good saturated fats like coconut oil, which contains medium chain triglycerides (MCT), which are beneficial in reducing your risk of developing heart disease and viable as body fuel that can be used immediately by your body. If you can drastically lower the amount of bad saturated fats and all trans fats from your diet, you're already on your way to avoiding serious heart diseases like artery buildup and strokes. So, enjoy some Fat's in your daily routine because they aren't all bad an instead try reducing or cutting out refined sugars, carbohydrates, and foods with a high glycemic load.

Carbohydrates

Carbohydrates are the fuel our bodies run on. Your body breaks down carbohydrates into glucose and stores them in you cells and tissues. They can even be stored in your muscles and liver for later use as energy. You'll find this macronutrient mainly in starchy foods like potatoes or fruits, milk, nuts, and seeds. Eating carbohydrates on a Paleo diet are necessary, but out of these foods the most preferred ones are those that are low in carbohydrate levels. Our normal diets consist of a large ratio of Carbohydrates in our daily routine. Paleo suggests differently; you're body should start using Fats instead of relying on Carbohydrates for fuel. This way you're able to burn Fat's and still supply you're body with the appropriate energy it needs. Apart from performing the job of a body fuel, Carbohydrates also cooperate with Fats in order to help get rid of bodily waste using the liver. Of course, we're talking in general terms, about the average person, with moderate activity levels per day consuming low levels of Carbohydrates. If you're an athlete you'll need a larger ratio of Carbohydrates in your system to perform well. This is an exception that is acceptable to Paleo. Performance athletes and people with higher activity levels all require a higher level of Carb's in their system and this is all achievable, even if you're on the Paleo diet.

Protein

Arguably, one of the most important macronutrients of all three, not that you can get by with just eating Proteins as discussed earlier, proteins can be harmful in large doses for longer periods if not well proportioned into ratios. Proteins are broken down by our body into essential amino acids, which our bodies themselves can make, but can also be burned as fuel when needed. Protein helps to build muscle mass, repair tissue, and strengthen the immune system. This is why you see athletes and sporty people consuming more protein content then normal people. Protein also helps to make important hormones and enzymes needed by the body. Animal meat has many essential amino acids and Vitamins like B-12 which is necessary for brain functions and can't be found in plant based proteins. This is why it's necessary to incorporate enough Protein in your diet to aid your essential body functions and keep up satiation levels. Eating more Proteins is one way to remain satiated so that you avoid making unhealthy diet choices. You can just replace that craving for bread, with some more meat on your plate. Like all the other macronutrients you need to be aware of what ratio of Protein is recommended for you age, sex, and activity levels.

- Children under 10 years of age, of average weight can benefit from about 46-54grams of Protein per day.

- Teenage boys, of average weight can benefit from 84-106grams of Protein per day.

- Teenage girls, of average weight can benefit from 74-84grams of Protein per day.

- Adult men of average weight can benefit from125-153grams of Protein per day.

- Adult women of average weight can benefit from 88-100grams of Protein per day.

There isn't really a magic formula for the ratio's that will tell you what's best. The recommended macronutrient ratios in most Paleo circles are 35% Protein, 20% Fats, and 45% Carbohydrates. The ratios can vary according to:

Your age: If you're over 35 you might not be able to consume the same amount of Fat and carbohydrates you used you at a younger age. Plus, your metabolism slows down after 30, and it's get a little harder to shed pounds after you put them on.

Your sex: If you're a man, you'll need more calories per day as compared to the average woman because men tend to have from muscle content as compared to women, who have more Fat content in their bodies. So, adjust the Fats, Carbohydrates, and Protein ratios according to the recommended calorie intake for your sex.

Your weight: Are you trying to lose weight? If yes, then a lower ratio of carbohydrates may help you achieve your goal. It's important to know what you're looking to achieve with Paleo. Diet changes can be helpful for autoimmune disorders and weight problems as well. Just make sure you opt for half a sweet potato instead of a full white potato portion. Reduce the number of calories you consume, lower you're Carbohydrates and Fats, and stick to low carbs and fats instead and you're body will start using you're Fat's as fuel, which means you'll burn more fat and replace it with muscle mass from the Protein you consume.

You're activity levels: Are you a stay at home mom? A university attending student, or a performance athlete? Because higher activity levels mean you'll need a macronutrient ratio that can provide you with higher muscle and energy levels in the long term. Tweak your protein and carbohydrate ratios to suit your needs.

You can use these websites for specific goals like weight loss, athletic performance, etc. to get an idea.

Weight loss: http://macronutrientcalculator.com/

http://www.caloriesperhour.com/tutorial_ratios.php

Body building:

http://www.bodybuilding.com/fun/macronutrients_calculator.htm

Chapter 2

Paleo approved food list – What foods are allowed on the Paleo diet

Here's a list of foods which are Paleo and should be included in your diet on a regular basis:

Animal meat (Go for leaner cuts, instead of fatty cuts): Pork, beef, lamb, chicken, turkey, rabbit, organ meats (heart, liver, kidney's), duck, , deer, elk, ostrich, wild turkey, venison, quail, pheasant, etc.

Fish: Wild salmon, mackerel, tuna, bass, swordfish, tilapia, red snapper, halibut, haddock, mullet, cod, etc.

Fats: Olive oil, coconut oil, avocado oil, macadamia nut oil, canola oil, grass fed ghee, grass fed butter, etc.

Shellfish: Oyster, crab, crayfish, lobster, prawns, mussels, scallops, clams, etc,

Vegetables: Artichokes, zucchini, squash, sweet potato, bell peppers, kale, celery, onion, pumpkin, broccoli, tomato, parsnips, cabbage, beets, brussel sprouts, collards, eggplant, cauliflower, radish, endive, watercress, mustard greens, carrots, etc.

Fruits: Apples, passion fruit, lemon, blackberries, strawberries, papaya, pears, pineapple, kiwi, apricot, banana, grapes, lychee, plums, nectarines, oranges, watermelon, mango, guava, etc.

Nuts and seeds: Almonds, macadamia nuts, pine nuts, pecans, cashews, pumpkin seeds, chestnuts, hazelnuts, brazil nuts, walnuts, etc.

Sweeteners: Raw honey, palm sugar, Grade B maple syrup, agave syrup, and chicory root.

A List of foods that aren't Paleo approved:

Starchy vegetables: white potatoes, yams, cassava root, tapioca, other starchy tubers.

Cereal grains: Barley, rice, millet, corn, oats, rye, wheat, sorghum, wild rice, amaranth, quinoa, buckwheat, and any processed foods made cereal grains.

Legumes: string beans, mung beans, garbanzo beans, peanuts, peas, lentils, snowpeas, etc.

Dairy: Milk, cheese, yoghurt, cream, ice cream, low fat milk, frozen yoghurt, cream cheese, etc.

Fats: All seed oils (sunflower, etc), trans fat, bad saturated fats, etc.

All sugar and sugary products: cakes, cookies, pies,

chocolates, ice creams, doughnuts, candy, etc.

Foods containing too much sodium: Bacon, salted nuts, hot dogs, processed meats, olives, dried or smoked deli meats, most canned fish and meats, salami, veggies, etc.

Other things not on the Paleo list: Fatty cuts of meats, sugary drinks and foods, energy drinks, all alcohol including beer.

Chapter 3

14 Day meal plan

Meal plans are a great way to make your transition to Paleo easier. As a diet, Paleo is exceptionally easy to follow because all of its ingredients are high quality and bursting with nutrients that will get you started on your Paleo journey to a healthier you. It may seem like an extra chore to create a meal plan and hang it where it's visible to you most of the time, but it can also be quite handy. For example, it's easier knowing ahead of time what you're going to cook, so that your shopping trip is a more efficient and cost effective, as opposed to just picking up things you think you want to eat, but may end up wasting or buying too much of.

Meal planning is also a great way to keep track of what you're eating on a daily basis. Especially, if you're noting down everything, from snacks to exercise routines; this will tell you where Paleo is most helpful to you (depending on your goal, whether it's weight loss, or relief from symptoms of autoimmune disorders), and where you need to make adjustments for a better result.

Being organized with your Paleo routine can help you tremendously when you're concerned about daily calorie intake. You can use the chart you make and calculate your daily calorific intake by analyzing recipes with calorie counting apps on your smart phones. This can help you in determining the right macronutrient ratio to consume. Don't fret if you don't get the ratio's correct the first time, make adjustments according to the recommended calorie intake for your age and sex; men and women need to consume a fairly different amount of calories daily. Where, men can get away with more calories than women because of their higher muscle mass as compared to women, who have more fat content in their bodies.

It's always helpful to have a plan if you want to succeed with Paleo. Paleo as a diet and lifestyle is simplistic in its applications and results, but due to the complexity of our current lifestyles and diet habits, it's better to keep a meal plan or even a food diary so that you can track what you're eating and how much activity you're getting in a week. Another important thing to keep in mind with your meal plan is to notice how the diet and activity over the weeks, affect your body and health. If you're proposed weekly routines are effective, you can further rely on it to give you optimum health and wellbeing in the long term, and it it's lacking somewhere, you can just make tweaks to ensure that you get the results you're looking for from Paleo.

This meal plan below is a sample meal plan; you can adjust it according to your needs.

1 Weeks Paleo meal plan

Saturday

Breakfast: Scrambled eggs and sausage

Snack: Kale smoothie

Exercise: 20 minutes low intensity aerobics

Lunch: Ahi tuna salad

Snack: Pear or apple

Dinner: Sweet chilli tilapia

Sunday

Breakfast: Veggie stir fry

Snack: Handful of Trail mix

Exercise: 15-20 minutes of slow paced walking

Lunch: lemon chicken and green beans

Snack: Green tea sweetened with raw honey

Dinner: Steak and mash with vegetables

Monday

Breakfast: Paleo oatmeal

Snack: 4-5 Strawberries dipped in dark chocolate.

Exercise: 15-20 minutes swimming laps

Lunch: Roasted purple cauliflower soup

Snack: Green tea sweetened with raw honey

Dinner: Lamb chops with sweet potato mash

Tuesday

Breakfast: Paleo breakfast muffin

Snack: Apple

Exercise: 20 minute Combination of cross fit exercises

Lunch: Chicken Caesar salad

Snack: Paleo salsa and carrot/celery sticks

Dinner: Paleo pizza

Wednesday

Breakfast: Fruit smoothie

Snack: Grapes

Lunch: Bacon wrapped asparagus and boiled eggs

Snack: cauliflower popcorn

Exercise: 5 minutes of going up walking up and down the stairs

Dinner: Meatballs and zucchini noodles

Thursday

Breakfast: Spinach omelet

Snack: Banana bread slice

Lunch: Boiled eggs and meat patties

Snack: Paleo granola bar

Exercise: 15-20 minutes slow paced walk

Dinner: Red thai curry

Friday

Breakfast: Paleo breakfast cookies

Snack: Watermelon

Exercise: 25 minutes of low intensity cardio

Lunch: Steak fajitas wrapped in lettuce leaves

Snack: Green tea and dark chocolate chips

Dinner: Paleo tomato and seafood pasta

2nd Weeks Paleo meal plan

Saturday

Breakfast: Scrambled egg whites with green beans

Snack: Baked sweet potato fries

Lunch: Turkey roll up with lettuce leaves and avocado slices

Snack: fruit smoothie

Exercise: 20 minutes low intensity aerobics

Dinner: Roast chicken with vegetables

Sunday

Breakfast: Eggs and sweet potato and bacon hash browns

Snack: Apple

Exercise: 15-20 minutes of slow paced walk

Lunch: Steamed salmon with broccoli and carrots

Snack: 2-3 Dark chocolate squares

Dinner: Ratatouille

Monday

Breakfast: Paleo chocolate chip pancakes

Snack: Pear slices with some nut butter

Exercise: 15-20 minute sprint

Lunch: Roasted red pepper soup

Snack: Green tea sweetened with raw honey

Dinner: Lamb chops with sweet potato mash

Tuesday

Breakfast: Paleo breakfast muffin

Snack: Apple slices with coconut butter

Exercise: Swimming

Lunch: Spinach and mushroom frittata

Snack: Fruit smoothie

Dinner: Eggplant lasagna

Wednesday

Breakfast: Fruit salad and mixed nuts

Snack: Paleo (gluten free) Chicken fingers

Exercise: 15 minute slow paced walk

Lunch: Bacon and egg cups

Snack: Green tea sweetened with raw honey

Dinner: Roast pork tenderloin

Thursday

Breakfast: Bacon and vegetable omelet

Snack: Paleo granola bar

Exercise: 15-20 minutes slow paced walk

Lunch: Chicken soup

Snack: Sliced almonds and berries

Dinner: Meat patties with avocado and olive salad

Friday

Breakfast: Bacon egg cups

Snack: Toasted almonds and nuts (handful)

Exercise: Cross fit exercises

Lunch: Seafood fajitas wrapped in lettuce leaves

Snack: Zucchini chips

Dinner: Asparagus risotto

Chapter 4

Recipes

Here are some delicious recipes, full of Paleo goodness to get you started on your way. You'll find that all of these recipes are simple to recreate and are full of Paleo approved ingredients. So, don't worry about not getting to eat your favorite foods again because you can recreate all those classic and common recipes using Paleo ingredients.

Week 1

Day 1

Breakfast

Almond strawberry pancakes

(Serves 4)

Ingredients

- ¾ cup almond flour
- 2 eggs
- ½ cup water

- 1 cup Strawberries (hulled and sliced thin)
- 1 tsp baking powder
- 1 tsp grade B maple syrup (more for pouring over pancakes)
- ½ tsp sea salt
- Olive oil or coconut oil to cook

Directions

1. Mix all of the pancake ingredients except for the strawberries and almonds in a bowl until you're sure the mixture is lump free.

2. Heat a little oil in a hot pan and make pancakes by dropping half a ladle of the mixture in the pan, cooking the pancakes on both sides, over low to medium heat for 3 minutes each, or until pancake is done and brown on both sides.

3. Serve hot with a garnish of strawberries and almond flakes on top.

Lunch

Roasted vegetables

(Serves 4)

Ingredients

2 cups Brussel sprouts (halved)

- 2 green bell peppers (optional)
- 1 sweet potato (peeled, cubed)
- 1 ½ pounds butternut squash (peeled, cubed)
- 1 pound smoked bacon
- 1 tablespoon vinegar
- 1 head of garlic
- 3 tbsp olive oil
- Sea salt and black pepper to taste

Directions

1 Pre-heat your oven to about 425 degrees F.

2 Steam the butternut squash, sweet potato, and brussel sprouts for 8 minutes, or until they're slightly tender.

3 Line two baking trays with some parchment paper and lay out the bacon strips evenly on one baking tray, and on another, add the brussel sprouts, green bell peppers (if using), sweet potato, and butternut squash drizzled with some olive oil, sea salt and pepper.

4 Cut the top off the head of the garlic and sprinkle with some olive oil, sea salt and pepper. Add it to one of baking tray before placing both of them in the oven for at least 18 minutes.

5 Take out the bacon when it's done and cut it into shorter strips and combine with vegetables in a

bowl.

6   Make the vinaigrette with 4-5 cloves from the garlic
you baked and mash it in with some sea salt, olive
oil, vinegar, black pepper and then drizzle over the
vegetables.

Dinner

Lamb chops with sweet potato mash

(Serves 2)

Ingredients for lamb chops:

- 250 g lamb chops (fat removed)
- 2-3 tbsp yoghurt (optional)
- 1 tsp ginger (minced)
- 2-3 garlic cloves (minced)
- 1 tsp paprika powder
- 1 tsp all spice powder
- 1 tsp sea salt
- 2 tbsp olive oil
- Juice of 1 lemon

Ingredients for mash:

- 1 large sweet potato
- 2-3 tbsp coconut milk
- 1 tbsp grass fed butter
- Sea salt and pepper to taste

Directions

1. Make a marinade for lamb chops by combining spices, yoghurt (optional), lemon juice, the minced garlic and ginger. Coat the lamb chops well in this marinade and then pour the marinade with the lamb chops in to a zip lock back, letting them refrigerate for 2-3 hours.

2. When you're ready to cook them, heat some olive oil in a pan and pan fry the lamb chops on both sides for about 7-8 minutes, or until they are tender and cooked through.

3. Make sweet potato mash by boiling the potato until it's soft enough, but not completely mushy.

4. Now mash together the boiled potatoes with some coconut milk (add it a tablespoon at a time), butter, sea salt and pepper, and mix until it's smooth as a mash should be.

5. Serve the lamb chops on a bed of sweet potato mash.

Dessert

Strawberry mousse

(Serves 4)

Ingredients

- 12-14 ripe strawberries
- 1 ripe avocado
- 2 ripe bananas
- 1 tsp vanilla extract
- ¼ tsp sea salt
- ½ cup of coconut oil (melted)
- 1 tablespoon grade B maple syrup

Directions

1. Add all the ingredients to a food processor and pulse in a food processor until completely smooth.

2. Pour into a bowl and keep in the fridge for an hour to set.

Day 2

Breakfast

Breakfast Paleo cookies

(Makes 1 dozen)

Ingredients

- 1/3 cup coconut flour
- 3-4 medjool dates (pitted)
- ½ cup applesauce (unsweetened)
- 1 tsp almond extract
- 1 tsp cacao powder
- 1 tsp baking soda
- 2 tbsp coconut oil
- ½ cup shredded coconut (unsweetened)
- 2 tbsp dried cranberries

Directions

1. Preheat you oven to 350 degrees F.

2. Put the dates, bananas, coconut oil, and applesauce in a food processor, pulsing until they become completely smooth. This can take 30 seconds.

3. Now slowly start adding the cacao powder, coconut flour, almond extract, baking soda, and process until its combined well.

4. Stir in the shredded coconut and cranberries.

5. Line a baking tray with some parchment paper and spoon golf ball sizes of the mixture onto the baking tray and flatten them slightly with a spoon, into the thickness you prefer.

6. Place them in the oven and let them bake for about 18-20 minutes until completely cooked.

7. You can store these in an airtight container.

Lunch

Warm Kale Salad with Bacon Dressing

(Serves 2)

Ingredients

- 4 slices bacon
- ½ a medium red onion (thinly sliced)
- 2 -3 tbsp apple cider vinegar
- 2 tablespoon dried currants
- baby kale (a medium bowlful)
- Sea salt and black pepper to taste

Directions

1 In a skillet, cook the bacon strips over medium low heat until they're crisp to your liking.

Paleo For Beginners

2 Now take out the bacon and add the onion and red currants in with the bacon fat in the skillet.

3 Let the onions soften up a bit and the currants become plump, a minute should be enough.

4 Now just add apple cider vinegar, then bring it to a simmer and turn off the heat.

5 Place the kale to a bowl, pouring over your warm dressing.

6 Chop up the cooked bacon and add to the bowl as well.

7 Season the salad with some sea salt and black pepper, tossing together gently before serving.

Dinner

Meatballs and zucchini noodles

(Serves 4-6)

Ingredients for meatballs and sauce:

- 500g beef mince
- 4 medium onions (chopped small)
- 1 chicken stock cube (low sodium)
- ¼ tsp all spice powder
- ½ tsp paprika powder

57

- Sea salt and black pepper to taste
- 2-3 tbsp olive oil
- Arrowroot powder

Ingredients for zucchini spaghetti:

4 zucchinis, 6 to 8 inches in size
Sea salt to taste
2 tbsp olive oil

Directions for meatballs:

1. Combine the minced meat, chopped onion, ¼ tsp sea salt, black pepper, and all spice powder in one bowl and mix these ingredients together well.

2. Start making medium sized meatballs from the mince meat mixture. Warm a skillet with a tablespoon of olive oil.

3. Fry the meatballs you made well on all sides, or until they are a nice brown.

4. Now, using the same skillet you browned the meatballs in, add 2 more tbsp of olive oil, and the chopped garlic on medium heat.

5. Once you start smelling the garlic, add rest of the onion, the chicken stock cube, ½ a cup of water mixed with a pinch of arrowroot powder, and the meatballs.

6. Let the meatballs cook for another 7-8 minutes, making sure they don't become too dry, or end up sticking to the bottom of the skillet.

7. You can add a pinch of oregano at the end to add some more flavor.

Directions for zucchini spaghetti:

1. Wash the zucchini well, peeling and coring the seeds. Then just julienne the zucchini hand into really thin spaghetti like strips.

2. Use another skillet and pour some olive oil in it. Once the skillet is heated, add half of the julienned zucchini. You can fry the spaghetti in two batches.

3. Add ¼ tsp of the sea salt, tossing and cooking the zucchini for 3 to 4 minutes, until just done. Repeat the same process with the remaining zucchini.

4. Pour the meatballs and sauce over the spaghetti and serve while it's hot.

Dessert

Coconut banana ice cream

(Serves 2)

Ingredients

- 1 mashed banana
- 2 tbsp grade B maple syrup
- 2 tsp vanilla extract
- 1 cup coconut cream (from top of coconut milk tin, when left in the fridge to chill)
- 1 can of coconut milk
- 1/3 cup coconut butter
- Dash of sea salt

Directions:

1. Add all the ingredients to a blender, except the coconut butter, and blend everything together really well, until smooth.

2. Pour the mixture into a churner (if you're using one) and churn the ice cream for at least 18 minutes before adding in the coconut butter.

3. Churn the ice cream for another 5 minutes, until it reaches the right consistency for an ice cream.

4. Scoop the ice cream out in to a plastic container with a lid, and keep frozen until serving.

Day 3

Breakfast

Breakfast Oatmeal

(Serves 1)

Ingredients:

4 tbsp chunky almond butter
2-3 tbsp coconut milk
1 ½ cups unsweetened applesauce
A handful of dried cranberries or dried apricots
Cinnamon to taste

Directions:

1. Over medium heat, combine all ingredients in a small pan, stirring often until thoroughly combined and warm.
2. Add the dried fruits you're using.

Lunch

Chicken and avocado lettuce Wraps with pineapple salsa

(Serves 2)

Ingredients:

- 1 ripe avocado (cut into slices)
- 1, 100g chicken breast (cut into long strips)
- 3-4 tbsp pineapple salsa
- 2-3 lettuce leaves
- 1 tablespoon olive oil
- Sea salt and black pepper

Directions:

1. Pour the oil in a hot pan, and add the chicken strips sautéing them until the chicken is cooked through well and browned.

2. Wash the lettuce leaves, and then blot them dry with clean a paper towel.

3. Assemble the wraps by adding a tablespoon or two of the chicken to a lettuce leaf and layer with a tablespoon of the salsa on top.

4. Wrap up the lettuce leaf with the filling and serve.

Eggplant Ragout

(Serves 6)

Ingredients

- 1 can of chickpeas (drained)
- 2 eggplants (deseeded, diced)
- 1 red onion (large, diced)
- 1 butternut squash (small, deseeded and diced)
- 1 can of tomatoes (drained, chopped)
- 2 yellow peppers (deseeded and diced)
- ½ tbsp tomato paste
- 4 cloves of garlic (chopped)
- 1 tsp all spice powder
- 1 tsp paprika powder
- 1 tsp turmeric powder
- 1 tsp sea salt
- 1 tsp palm sugar
- Black pepper to taste
- 3 tbsp olive oil
- 4-5 sprigs of parsley

Directions

1. In a medium sized pot, heat some olive oil and add garlic to it.

2. When you smell the garlic, add the onion to it and stir until slightly sautéed.

3. Now add the tomatoes, chickpeas, eggplant, bell peppers, squash, paprika powder, sea salt, turmeric powder, palm sugar, and tomato paste.

4. Cover and cook over low heat, until the eggplant is cooked, but not completely mushy.

5. Serve with some parsley and a little all spice powder.

Dessert

Chocolate brownies

(Serves 8)

Ingredients:

- 3 eggs
- 2 large, ripe avocados
- 4 oz baking chocolate (65% cocoa at least)
- ¼ cups cocoa powder (unsweetened)
- ½ cup raw honey or grade B maple syrup
- ½ tsp baking powder
- 1 tbsp almond flour
- 1 tbsp vanilla extract
- ½ cup crushed walnuts
- 1 tbsp coconut oil
- ½ tsp sea salt

Directions:

1. Pre-heat your oven to 325 degrees F.

2. Melt the chocolate and coconut oil in your microwave for about 20 seconds and remember to stir it constantly so that it doesn't end up curdling.

3. Mash the avocados with a fork, or just process them in a food processor and make sure no lumps remain.

4. Now add the avocados to the chocolate and coconut oil mixture.

5. Now slowly start adding the other ingredients while blending well. Add the walnuts to the batter at the end after coating them in a little flour, and folding them in.

6. Pour the batter you prepared into an already greased 8x8 inch pan and place it in the oven for 30 minutes.

7. Take them out of the oven and leave them to cool properly before serving.

Day 4

Breakfast

Paleo porridge

(Serves 2-4)

Ingredients

- 2 ripe bananas (mashed)
- 1 can of coconut milk
- ¼ cup flax meal
- ¾ cup almond meal
- 1 tsp cinnamon
- 1/8 tsp nutmeg powder
- 1 pinch sea salt
- 1 tablespoon raw honey (optional)
- Some unsweetened coconut flakes, nuts, berries seeds, etc (optional)

Directions:

1 Mix all the ingredients in a saucepan over low heat and let it simmer, stirring all the while, until it becomes thick.

2 Depending on what coconut milk you use, the mixture may seem thin at first, but it will thicken up quickly.

3   After you take it off heat, it may continue to thicken up and you can add water to make it a thinner consistency. Garnish with shredded coconut, nuts, and dried fruit if you like.

Lunch

Chicken Soup

(Serves 4)

Ingredients:

- 3-4, 100g chicken breasts
- 8 cloves of garlic (chopped)
- 1 14-oz. can diced tomatoes.
- 2 sweet potatoes (peeled, diced)
- 2 cups red cabbage (thinly shredded)
- 1 yellow summer squash (diced)
- 1 green bell pepper (deseeded, diced)
- 2 zucchini's (deseeded, diced)
- 1 4-oz. can chopped green chilies
- 1 tsp oregano
- 1 tsp parsley
- 2 or more cups chicken broth, as needed
- A dash or two of balsamic vinegar to taste
- Sea salt and freshly ground pepper to taste
- Olive oil, as needed

Directions:

1. Drizzle some olive oil in a slow cooker and put the chicken breasts in it, with half the garlic. Season a little with sea salt and pepper.
2. In a bowl, combine the bell pepper, zucchini, cabbage, sweet potatoes, and green chillies, tossing them with another drizzle of olive oil. Season the mixture with sea salt, black pepper, oregano, and toss to coat.
3. Pour the veggie mix into the crock pot, in an even layer. Add in the chicken broth, tomatoes, and a small dash of balsamic vinegar, to taste.
4. The liquid content should just about cover the veggies in the pot. If you like, you can add more broth to get a better consistency of a soup.
5. Cover the pot and let it cook for up to 5 to 6 hours, or until the chicken is tender and easily pulls apart into pieces.

Dinner

Baked Sweet Chili Tilapia

(Serves 2)

Ingredients:

- 2, 100g tilapia fillets
- 5 tbsp apple cider vinegar

- 3 minced red chilies
- 1 inch minced ginger
- 2-3 cloves minced garlic
- 2 tbsp grade B maple syrup
- 2 shredded carrots
- ¼ tsp sea salt
- 2 thin slices of lemon
- Some olive oil
- Parchment paper (Enough to wrap the fish inside)

Directions:

1. Pre-heat oven to 375 degrees F.

2. Marinate the fish fillets with all the above ingredients and cut some parchment paper 13 x 9 inches in size. Lay the lemon slices crosswise on it and then place one of the fish fillets in the center and wrap it up in the parchment paper properly.

3. Bake for about 25 minutes, the fish should flake easily.

Dessert

Coconut blueberry chia pudding

(Serves 3-4)

Ingredients

- 1½ cups coconut milk
- ¼ cup chia seeds
- 1 tbsp grade B maple syrup
- ⅓ cup frozen blueberries (thawed)
- ½ tsp vanilla extract
- ¼ tsp almond extract
- 2 tbsp shredded unsweetened coconut
- Pinch of sea salt

Directions

1. In a medium bowl mix together the coconut milk, chia seeds, sea salt, maple syrup, and vanilla extract.

2. Cover the bowl with some plastic wrap and let it refrigerate for at least 3 hours.

3. Serve, once the pudding has thickened, spooning into bowls and top with blueberries, some shredded coconut and more maple syrup if needed.

Day 5

Breakfast

Bacon and egg cups

(Makes 12 cups)

Ingredients

- 1 dozen eggs
- 12 bacon rashers
- Butter (for greasing)
- Handful of spinach
- Sea salt and black pepper to taste
- 1 mini muffin pan

Directions

1. Preheat your oven to 400 F.

2. Cut the bacon into even strips, save the broken bits to put in the bottom of the muffin pan.

3. Grease your muffin pan with any butter, or any other fat.

4. Use the strips of bacon to make walls of the muffin cup, place a broken off bit at the bottom and use the strips to make the cups.

5. Put the muffin tin in the oven for 5 minutes, allowing the bacon to cook slightly.

6. Now take out the muffin tin and sprinkle some feta into each cup, crack an egg in each of these cups.

7. Bake these cups for 10-15 minutes, until the eggs are firm, serve with some spinach and cracked black pepper.

Lunch
Zucchini Pasta with tomato Sauce

(Serves 1)

Ingredients

- 1 zucchini (cut into thin pasta shape)
- 1 large onion (diced)
- 2 large tomatoes (diced)
- ½ cup stock (chicken)
- ¼ tsp paprika powder
- ¼ tsp ginger (minced)
- ¼ tsp oregano
- 2 tsp of olive oil
- Sea salt and black pepper to taste
- Squeeze of lemon juice

Directions

1 Heat a pan with some olive oil over medium heat.

2 Add the julienned zucchini to the pan sautéing for about 3-4 minutes, or just until the zucchini has softened up, but is still firm. Stir often and carefully not breaking the zucchini.

3 While the zucchini is cooking, carve an X at the bottom of both tomatoes and let them boil for five minutes. When they've cooled, peel off the skin from the tomatoes and chop them up roughly.

4 In another pan, use some olive oil and add the onion and chopped tomatoes with ginger, sea salt, black pepper, and paprika powder, stirring well and often. Keep the heat on medium, so you don't burn the sauce, but hot enough to dry up excess water from the tomatoes.

5 Once the tomatoes have or cooked down, add the chicken stock and let the sauce simmer for 5-7 minutes, over a low flame.

6 Serve the sauce on a bed of zucchini spaghetti, or just mix the sauce into the pan with the spaghetti, sprinkling some oregano over it before you serve.

Dinner
Stuffed Peppers
(Serves 6-8)

- 1 lb chicken mince
- 8 bell peppers, with their tops cut off and deseeded (red and yellow)
- ½ cups red onion (finely chopped)
- 2 tsps cumin powder
- 1 tsp red chili powder
- ¼ tsp all spice powder
- 1 cup cilantro (finely chopped)
- 1 tsp sea salt

Directions

1 Preheat your oven to 350° F.

2 In a bowl mix the chicken mince, with onion, cilantro, chilli powder, cumin and salt

3 Now cut all the tops off of the peppers, deseeding them carefully and set aside.

4 Place the peppers in an appropriate sized dish..

5 Spoon the chicken mixture in the hollowed out peppers the peppers, place the tops back on.

6 Bake the stuffed peppers for 1 hour.

7   Let them rest for a few minutes after you taken them out of the oven.

8   Serve hot.

Dessert

Grilled Peaches with Coconut Cream

Ingredients

- 1 can coconut milk (refrigerated)
- 1/4 cup chopped walnuts
- 3 medium ripe peaches (cut in half with pit removed)
- 1 tsp vanilla extract
- Cinnamon (to taste)

Directions

1. Place peaches on a grill, cut side down first. Grill them on a medium-low heat until they're soft. This will be about 3-5 minutes on each side.

2. Scoop the cream off the top of the can of chilled coconut milk and whip it with vanilla extract using a handheld mixer.

3. Drizzle the coconut cream over each peach and top with some powdered cinnamon and chopped walnuts to serve.

Day 6

Breakfast
Spinach omelet
(Serves 2)

Ingredients

- 2 eggs
- 1 pinch of paprika powder
- Cheese (optional)
- Handful of spinach leaves (washed, chopped)
- Sea salt to taste
- ½ tablespoon olive oil

Directions

1. Heat a medium skillet with some olive oil.

2. Beat the eggs together with some sea salt, paprika powder and cheese (if using).

3. Now pour the egg mixture into the hot skillet and sprinkle some spinach over it.

4. Let the omelette cook at the bottom and then flip over to cook the other side as well.

Lunch

Chicken tacos

(Serves 2)

Ingredients

- 1lbs boneless chicken breast (cut into thin strips)
- 1 red onion (diced)
- 2 tomatoes, (diced)
- 1 jalapeno (minced)
- ½ cup chicken broth
- ¼ tsp sea salt
- ¼ tsp black pepper
- 4-5 large lettuce leaves
- 3 tbsp lime juice
- 1tbsp olive oil

Directions

1. Start by seasoning the chicken with sea salt, black pepper, and lime juice
2. Using a large pan on medium-high, sauté until the chicken is slightly browned, which should take roughly 4-5 minutes.
3. Remove the chicken from pan now and place in a bowl to set aside.
4. Add the onion and jalapeno to it, cooking until onions are a bit translucent and jalapeno is tender. Then add the broth and tomatoes to it.

5. Let it simmer on lower the heat for about 2-3 minutes and be sure to continually stir, and scrap the sides to get everything to cook evenly.
6. Add the chicken back into mixture and then pour in the lime juice.
7. Let it simmer until, your chicken is cooked all the way through.
8. Lay out some lettuce leaves (washed and blotted dry), and place some of the meat mixture in the center.
9. Top with any added vegetables, and wrap up.

Dinner

Paleo meatloaf

(Serves 8)

Ingredients

- 2 eggs
- 1½ lbs beef mince
- 4 oz tomato sauce (sugar free/gluten free)
- 1/3 cup crushed pork skins (fried)
- 1 tbsp worcestershire sauce
- 2½ tsp paprika powder
- 1 ½ tsp all spice powder
- 1 tbsp garlic salt
- 1 tbsp garlic pepper seasoning

Directions

1. Preheat the oven to 375 degrees F.
2. In a large bowl, whisk together eggs with beef mince, fried pork skin, tomato sauce and worcestershire sauce.
3. Season the mixture with paprika powder, garlic salt and garlic pepper and mix until well incorporated.
4. Form the mixture into a proper loaf and place onto a greased loaf pan.
5. Let the meat loaf bake for about 35 to 40 minutes.
6. Allow the loaf to stand for 5 minutes before cutting into it.
7. Slice and serve

Dessert

Coconut strawberry pudding

(Serves 3-4)

Ingredients

- 1½ cups coconut milk (refrigerated)
- ½ cup frozen strawberries (thawed)
- ¼ tsp almond extract
- 1 tbsp grade B maple syrup
- 2 tbsp shredded coconut
- 1 tbsp almond flakes
- Pinch of sea salt

Directions

1. In a medium bowl whisk together the coconut milk, maple syrup, sea salt, and almond extract in a bowl.

2. Cover the bowl with some plastic cling wrap and let it refrigerate for at least 3 hours.

3. Serve, once the pudding has thickened, spooning into serving bowls and topping with fresh strawberries, some shredded coconut, almond flakes, and even more maple syrup if needed.

Day 7

Breakfast

Blueberry breakfast smoothie

(Serves 1)

Ingredients:

- 1 banana (peeled and chopped)
- 1 cup strawberries
- ½ cup blueberries
- ½ cup orange juice
- 1 kiwi (sliced)
- 8 oz peach yogurt (or use almond milk instead)
- 1 cup ice cubes

Directions:

1. Combine the peach yogurt (if using) in a blender with the blueberries, strawberries, banana, kiwi, orange juice, and some ice cubes.

2. Blend together until smooth.

3. Serve!

Lunch

Grilled Portobello mushrooms

(Serves 3)

Ingredients:

- 4 garlic cloves (minced)
- 3 Portobello mushrooms (cleaned and stem less)
- 3 tbsp red onions (chopped)
- 4 tbsp balsamic vinegar
- ¼ cup olive oil

Directions:

1. In a mixing bowl, combine the olive oil with onions, minced garlic, and vinegar.

2. Spoon the mixture evenly into the mushroom caps and let it stand for an hour.

3. Grill the mushroom caps over a hot grill for approximately 10 minutes.

4. Serve immediately!

Dinner

Baked Salmon
(Serves 2)

Ingredients:

- 8 oz. salmon fillet
- 1 garlic clove
- 1 chopped tomato
- ½ chopped red onion
- 1 tsp apple cider vinegar
- ½ tsp paprika powder
- ¼ tsp sea salt
- ¼ tsp cumin
- 1 jalapeno pepper

Directions:

1. Preheat the oven to 400 degrees F.
2. While the oven is heats up, process the sea salt, cumin, paprika powder, vinegar, jalapeno, garlic, onion, and tomato in a food processor until they become finely chopped.
3. Place the salmon into a roasting pan before spooning your mixture from the food processor on top.
4. Place the roasting pan into the oven and let the salmon bake for about 15 minutes, making sure the fish is cooked all the way through.
5. Serve with your favorite vegetables and sauce.

Dessert

Raspberry lime popsicles

(Serves 10)

Ingredients

- 1/4 cup lime juice
- ¼ tsp of raw honey
- 3 cups ripe pineapple (chopped)
- 1 cup raspberries
- pinch of sea salt
- popsicle moulds

Directions

1. Blend all the ingredients together well and then pour into popsicle molds, letting them freeze for 6 hours.

Week 2

Day 8

Breakfast

(Makes 1 mini loaf)

Paleo date and walnut bread

Ingredients

- 3 large eggs
- 2 tbsp coconut flour
- ½ cup almond flour
- ¼ tsp baking soda
- ¼ almond extract
- A pinch of cinnamon powder
- 1 tablespoon apple cider vinegar
- 3 large medjool dates pitted
- ⅛ tsp sea salt
- ½ cup chopped walnuts

Directions:

1. Preheat your oven to 350 degree F.

2. Process together the almond flour and coconut flour, baking soda, and sea salt in a food processor.

3. Now add the medjool dates and process again, until well incorporated. The mixture should resemble

coarse sand.

4. Now add in the eggs, almond extract and apple cider vinegar, briefly pulsing with the chopped walnuts.

5. Pour the batter into a prepared mini load pan..

6. Bake the mini loaf for about 30-32 minutes or until the loaf is baked through.

7. Let it cool in the pan itself for at least 2 hours before turning out.

Lunch

Roasted cauliflower soup

(Serves 3-4)

Ingredients

- 1 purple cauliflower head (large)
- 1 large red onion (diced)
- 4 cups stock (chicken)
- 2-3 cloves garlic
- 1 tsp paprika powder
- 4 tbsp olive oil .

Directions

1 Preheat your oven to 350° F.
2 Rub the cauliflower head with some olive oil, paprika powder, and sea salt before placing the entire head

in a large baking dish. Roast the garlic cloves with the cauliflower in the last 20-25 minutes.

3 Add ½ a cup of water to the baking dish before placing it in the oven to bake uncovered for at least 1 ½ hours, or until your knife can cut through the cauliflower's core easily.

4 After removing from the oven let it cool for a while, before chopping up coarsely.

5 Add the chopped cauliflower and garlic to a food processor with the chicken stock and process until completely smooth.

6 Now pour the soup into a saucepan and season with sea salt and black pepper and heat through properly and garnish with some coconut cream before serving.

Dinner

Paleo pizza

(Makes a 6 inch diameter pizza)

Ingredients

Crust
- 1 ¼ cup almond flour
- 2 egg whites
- 3 cups cauliflower (ground in a food processor, it should look like rice)
- 1 tsp garlic powder
- 1 tsp sea salt

Tomato sauce
- 1 tsp oregano
- 4 garlic cloves (minced)
- 4 large tomatoes (boiled, peeled)
- Salt and pepper to taste

Toppings
- 1 red bell pepper (medium, julienned)
- 1 white onion (medium, sliced thin)
- 1 chicken breast (grilled or cooked and cut into bite sized pieces)
- 7-8 rashes of bacon
- 1 jalapeno pepper (sliced thick)

Directions

1. Pre-heat your oven to 450 degrees and line your baking tray with parchment paper.

2. Mix all the ingredients in a bowl for the crust and combine them until a thick, dough forms.

3. Take about a cup of the mixture you made and use this to make your pizza crust on a baking tray, spreading it out into a circle of uniform thickness.

4. First bake your pizza crusts without the toppings for 20 minutes, until they look browned slightly.

5. Next, take all the ingredients for the tomato sauce

and blend them in a blender, until smooth.

6. Add the toppings, after a liberal spreading of the tomato sauce on the crust and put the pizza back in the oven for another 10 minutes to cook the top.

Dessert

Blueberry cream pie

(Serves 8-10)

Ingredients

Crust:
- ½ cup raw honey
- 3 cups almonds
- 2 tbsp coconut oil
- 1 tbsp lemon zest
- 1 tsp almond extract
- ½ tsp cinnamon
- A pinch of sea salt

Filling:
- 4 cups blueberries for serving
- 1 can coconut milk (chilled)
- 2 tsp plant-based gelatine (dissolved in 2 tbsp hot water)
- ⅓ cup freshly squeezed lemon juice
- ⅓ cup raw honey

Directions

1. Process the cinnamon and almonds in a food processor until a crumbly texture is reached.
2. Add rest of the crust ingredients and process again until a sticky dough forms. Press the crust firmly into a pie plate, using a little water to keep your hands from sticking to the crust.
3. For the pie filling, mix the gelatine and water together until completely dissolved and then immediately add the lemon juice. In case the gelatine gets lumpy, keep the mixture over hot water until it melts.
4. Pour the coconut milk into an electric mixer, adding raw honey and then whipping on high speed until stiff peaks form. This can take about 15 minutes. Add the gelatine mixture to the prepared whipped cream and then pour this filling into the pie crust.
5. The filling will set properly in the refrigerator.
6. After letting the pie chill for at least 4-5 hours or until set, serve with lots of blueberries on top.

Day 9

Breakfast

Fruit salad and mixed nuts

(Serves 1)

Ingredients

- Any seasonal fruits (kiwis, berries, pineapple, apples, mangoes, pomegranate, etc.)
- 1 tablespoon grade B maple syrup
- 1 tsp almond slivers
- A pinch of cinnamon or all spice powder

Directions

1. Cut the fruits into small bite sized pieces and drizzle with maple syrup, almonds, and cinnamon powder if using.

Lunch

Chicken Cranberry Salad

Serves 3

Ingredients:

- 1 lbs boneless chicken (boiled)
- ½ cup cranberries (dried)

91

- 1 cup green grapes (halved)
- 1 apple (peeled, cored, and chopped)
- 1 cup celery (chopped)
- 1 cup Paleo mayonnaise
- 1 ½ tsp lemon juice
- Sea salt and black pepper (to taste)

Directions:

1. In a large bowl combine the chicken with the cranberries, grapes, apple, and celery, tossing it thoroughly.

2. In another bowl, mix the mayonnaise with the lemon juice, sea salt and black pepper.

3. Pour the dressing over the chicken mixture and incorporate well.

4. Serve warm or cold.

Dinner

Salmon and Asparagus with Tomato Salsa

(Serves 4)

Ingredients:

Salmon:
- 4 salmon fillets (with skin)
- 1 tsp lemon juice

- 1 tsp lemon zest
- 2 garlic cloves (minced)
- ½ tsp red chilli powder
- ½ tsp ground black pepper
- ½ tsp sea salt
- 1 tsp olive oil

Roasted Asparagus:
- 1 bunch of asparagus
- ¼ tsp garlic powder
- ½ tsp lemon juice
- 1 tbsp olive oil
- ¼ tsp sea salt
- ¼ tsp black pepper

Tomato Salsa:
- ½ cup cherry tomatoes (each cut into 4 pieces)
- 2 garlic cloves (minced)
- ½ tsp paprika powder
- 1 tsp lemon zest
- 1 tsp lemon juice
- ¼ cup oregano (freshly chopped)
- ¼ tsp sea salt
- ¼ tsp ground black pepper
- 2 tbsp olive oil

Directions:

Salmon:
1. Preheat the oven to 400 degrees F.
2. In a bowl, mix the garlic, lemon juice, lemon zest, paprika, sea salt, pepper, and olive oil.
3. Thoroughly rub the mixture on both sides of the salmon, allowing it to marinade overnight.
4. Line a baking sheet and place the marinated salmon on it. Broil the fish for about 10-12 minutes or until it turns pink and flaky.

Roasted Asparagus:
1. Preheat the oven to 400F.
2. Remove the top of the asparagus stalks and spread the asparagus on a large baking sheet.
3. Drizzle the asparagus with olive oil, lemon juice on it followed by sea salt, pepper and garlic.
4. Bake them for approximately 5 minutes and then flip and bake for another 5 minutes.

Tomato Salsa:
1. Whisk together the garlic, lemon zest, lemon juice, olive oil, sea salt and black pepper in a small bowl.
2. Add cherry tomatoes to this and mix well.
3. Pour the salsa over the cooked salmon and serve.

Dessert

Ingredients

Crust:

- 1/4 cup almond butter
- 1 cup almond flour
- 1 tbsp unsweetened maple syrup
- 1 tbsp grass-fed butter (softened)
- 1 tsp vanilla extract
- 1/2 tsp baking powder
- 1/4 tsp sea salt

Filling:

- 3 eggs
- ½ cup raw honey
- 2 1/2 tbsp coconut flour
- ¼ cup lemon juice
- 1 tbsp lemon zest, finely grated
- Pinch of sea salt

Directions:

1. Preheat your oven to 350 degrees F and grease a 9×9 inch baking dish with coconut oil or butter.
2. Combine all of the crust ingredients in food processor until a "crumbly" texture forms.
3. Press the crust firmly and evenly into the bottom of the pie dish. Using a fork, prick a few holes into

crust.

4. Bake the pie crust for 10 minutes and then take out of the oven.
5. While the pie crust bakes, mix all filling ingredients in a food processor until well incorporated together.
6. When the filling is ready, remove crust from oven and pour filling evenly into the crust. Continue baking the pie for 15-20 minutes, or until the filling is set, but still jiggles a little.
7. Cool completely on wire rack or chill in your fridge.

Dessert

Dark chocolate pudding

(Serves 4)

Ingredients

- 4 tbsp raw cacao powder
- 2 large ripe bananas
- ½ cup of melted coconut butter
- 1 large avocado
- 2 tbsp grade B maple syrup
- ½ tsp vanilla extract
- ¼ tsp sea salt

Directions:

1 Add all of the above ingredients into a processor and process until a smooth texture forms.
2 Pour the pudding into a bowl and let it chill for 2 hours.

Day 10

Breakfast

Apple, bacon and butternut squash hash

(Serves 2)

Ingredients

- 1 cup apples (diced)
- 4-5 strips bacon
- ¼ cup green onions (chopped)
- 2 cups butternut squash (diced, cooked)
- ½ tsp sea salt
- Black pepper to taste

Directions

1 Heat a skillet over medium heat and add bacon, cooking till crispy. After it cools, break into pieces. Leave the bacon fat in the skillet for frying the squash.
2 Now add all the butternut squash and apples to the bacon fat and continue to cook the hash over medium high heat until the apples just begin to soften. Make sure you don't stir too much and spread the squash and apples evenly over the skillet so that they brown nicely.
3 After removing from the heat, add the bacon pieces, green onion and the seasonings.

Lunch

Waldorf salad

(Serves 4)

Ingredients:

- 2 apples (cored and sliced)
- 1 cup green grapes (fresh)
- 1 cup boneless chicken (boiled, optional)
- 1 cup walnuts (rough chopped)
- 1 cup celery (diced)
- ¼ cup green onion
- Romaine lettuce leaves
- 7 tbsp Paleo mayonnaise
- 2 tbsp lemon juice
- ¼ tsp sea salt
- ¼ tsp ground black pepper

Directions:

1. Whisk together the mayonnaise and the lemon juice in a mixing bowl. Season it with some sea salt and black pepper.
2. Add the apples, celery, walnuts onions, grapes and chicken (optional) and mix well.
3. Serve cold over a bed of lettuce.

Dinner

Mushroom Shallot Frittata

(Serves 4)

Ingredients:
- 3 eggs
- 5 large egg whites
- 4 shallots (finely chopped)
- ½ pounds mushrooms (finely chopped)
- 2 tsp fresh parsley (chopped)
- 1 tbsp unsalted butter
- Black pepper to taste
- 1 tablespoon almond milk

Directions:
1. Preheat the oven to 350 degrees F.
2. Heat the butter in a large oven-proof skillet over medium heat and stir in shallots, sautéing until golden. This will take about 5 minutes.
3. Add in chopped mushrooms, parsley, and black pepper.
4. In a bowl whisk together eggs, egg whites, and almond milk. Add the egg mixture to the skillet, letting the eggs cover all the mushrooms.
5. When the edges begin to set in about 2 minutes, move the skillet to the oven, letting it bake for 15 minutes, or until the frittata is completely cooked.
6. Serve warm, cutting into 4 equal wedges.

Dessert
Raspberry and chocolate cupcake

(Serves 8)

Ingredients

- 4 eggs
- 1 cup almond flour
- ¼ cup coconut flour
- 2 tbsp. vanilla extract
- 3 tbsp. melted butter
- ¼ cup grade B maple syrup
- 1 cup frozen raspberries + tbsp. of almond flour

Directions

1 Pre-heat your oven to 375 degrees F.
2 Combine all the above ingredients in a bowl except for the raspberries and a tablespoon of almond flour.
3 In another bowl add the raspberries tossing them with a tablespoon of almond flour before adding them to your cake batter, folding them in.
4 Using an ice cream scoop, scoop the batter into your cupcake tin, filling ¼ of each.
5 Bake the cupcakes for 15-20 minutes, until they turn slightly golden brown and you stick a tooth pick in the center and it comes out clean.
6 Cool down the cupcakes for at least 15 minutes before frosting them, or just enjoy as they are.

Day 11

Breakfast

Breakfast Burrito

(Serves 2)

Ingredients

- 2 egg whites (large)
- 1 red onion (small, chopped)
- 2, 10 inch tortilla's (paleo, gluten free)
- 1 cup spinach leaves (washed)
- ½ cup of homemade salsa (Paleo)
- 1 tbsp olive oil

Directions

1. Heat a skillet with some non stick spray and make scrambled eggs with your favourite seasonings (sea salt, pepper, or paprika if desired) and the spinach and onions, sautéing until the spinach is a bit wilted and egg whites are totally scrambled.

Lunch

Szechuan chicken

(Serves 4)

Ingredients

- 1 boneless chicken breast (cut into 1-inch pieces)
- 1/2 cup carrots (matchstick-cut)
- 8 oz mushrooms (chopped)
- 2 cups black bean sauce (gluten free)
- 1 tablespoon ginger (minced)
- 1 tablespoon coconut aminos
- 1/2 cup green onions (chopped)
- 1 tsp arrowroot powder
- ½ cup chicken stock
- 1/4 tsp salt
- 1 tbsp olive oil
- Cooking spray

Directions

1 Broil chicken until it's nice and golden.
2 While the chicken is cooking, whisk together your chicken stock, black bean sauce, coconut aminos, and arrow root powder; set aside.
3 To a heated skillet, add the olive oil and mushrooms with sea salt, sautéing until the liquid dries up, this should take about 4 minutes.
4 Now stir in carrots and ginger, cooking for 1 minute. Add the sauce mixture and cook for another 30 seconds or at least until the sauce begins to thicken.
5 Now just remove from heat and stir in the chicken and onions.
6 Serve hot, with a sprinkle of peanuts on top.

Dinner

Paleo Shepherd's Pie

(Serves 8)

Ingredients

- 1 pound organic grass fed ground beef
- 1 pound turkey (cut into 2 inch slices)
- 1 cup chicken broth
- 1 large red onion (diced)
- 2 large heads cauliflower
- 2 cups diced carrots
- 2 cups diced celery
- ½ tsp sea salt
- 1 tsp black pepper
- ½ tsp smoked paprika
- 2 tbsp olive oil

Directions

1. Heat some olive oil in a very large frying pan and sauté the onion for 15 minutes until soft.
2. Add bacon pieces to pan and sauté until cooked, about 10 minutes.
3. Add carrots and celery to pan and sauté in bacon fat for 10 minutes until soft.
4. Add ground beef to pan and sauté until brown for just a few minutes.

5. Season with sea salt, black pepper, and smoked paprika.
6. Add chicken stock and let it cook down until a little more than half has evaporated.
7. Put the cauliflower in the food processor and puree with some olive oil until smooth.
8. Pour the ground beef mixture into a 9x13 inch baking dish and scoop on the cauliflower mixture over it.
9. Bake at 350 degrees F for 30 minutes.
10. Let it stand for 5-10 before cutting in and serving.

Dessert

Black Forrest Shake

(Serves 2)

Ingredients

- ½ a banana
- 1 cup pitted, fresh cherries (if not available, used canned)
- 2 tbsp unsweetened cocoa powder
- 1/8 vanilla extract
- 1 cup almond milk
- Dark chocolate and coconut shavings

Directions

1. Blend all the above ingredients in a blender until well incorporated and then garnish with dark chocolate and coconut shavings.

Day 12

Breakfast

Paleo cereal

(Serves 2)

Ingredients

- 2 tbsp grass fed butter
- 3 ½ cups unsweetened coconut flakes
- 2 tbsp cinnamon
- 4 tbsp palm sugar

Directions

1. Preheat the oven to 350 degrees F.
2. In a saucepan, over medium heat, add the butter, cinnamon, and palm sugar, heating until thoroughly incorporated.
3. Place the coconut flakes in a large bowl and pour the sauce over the coconut flakes and stir to coat well.
4. Now spread the coconut flakes onto a rimmed baking sheet.
5. Bake the flakes for 5-8 minutes, flipping the coconut every few minutes so they don't burn.
6. Allow the coconut to cool and serve with some cold almond or coconut milk.

Lunch

Taco Salad

(Serves 4-6)

Ingredients

- 1 lbs ground turkey
- 1 avocado (pitted, diced)
- 1 bell pepper (large, any color)
- 1 packet taco seasoning (low sodium)
- 1 bag romaine lettuce (chopped small)
- 1 can black olives (sliced)
- 1-2 tomatoes (seeded, diced)
- 1 cucumber (seeded, diced)
- Paleo salsa (no sugar added)

Directions

1. Over medium-high heat, brown the turkey mince.
2. Add the taco seasoning to it and a 1 tablespoon of water to the skillet when the meat is totally brown, stirring well, until well combined.
3. While the meat is cooking and prepare all the veggies.
4. To serve, layer the lettuce, turkey, and vegetables as you please.
5. Add the salsa as desired.

Dinner

Chicken Piccata

(Serves 4)

Ingredients

- 2 onions (chopped)
- 4 chicken breasts (skinless, boneless)
- 2 cups artichoke hearts (chopped)
- 2 cloves of garlic (minced)
- 3 tablespoon capers
- ½ cup lemon juice
- 1 tbsp black pepper
- 1 cup chicken stock
- 3 tbsp olive oil

Directions

1. In a shallow dish, mix together chicken stock, chicken, with lemon juice, leaving it to marinate overnight in the refrigerator.
2. In a pan, heat oil and adding garlic and onion, letting them sauté for about 2 minutes.
3. When you're ready to cook, take the chicken out from the marinade, saving the marinade.
4. Cook the chicken on each side for 5-10 minutes, or until browned.
5. Add in the black pepper, artichoke hearts, and the

marinade you saved.

6. Now just lower the heat, letting it simmer until the chicken is cooked through, for about another 10 minutes.

Dessert

Dark chocolate (make sure It's at least 70% or more cocoa)

Day 13

Breakfast

Scrambled eggs with carrots and zucchini

(Serves 2)

Ingredients

- 5 eggs
- 2 carrots (peeled and grated)
- 2 zucchinis (peeled and grated)
- 1 tablespoon coconut aminos
- ¼ tsp paprika powder
- Sea salt and black pepper to taste
- 2 tablespoons olive oil

Directions

1. Stir-fry the carrots and zucchinis with tablespoon of olive oil over medium heat in a skillet, stirring often to make sure none of it sticks to the pan.

2. Add the other tablespoon of olive oil to a saucepan on a medium heat and just crack all the eggs into the saucepan. Stir the eggs with a spatula to break them apart in the pan. Just don't bother whisking the eggs beforehand.

3. Keep stirring the eggs on a low to medium heat to

make the eggs scrambled.

4. When the eggs are still moist but fairly solid, add some sea salt and black pepper to the eggs, taking them off the heat.

5. Add a tablespoon of coconut aminos salt and pepper to the carrots and zucchinis putting them into the bottom of each bowl and topping with some of the scrambled eggs.

Lunch

Beef and Veggie Wrap

(Serves 2)

Ingredients:

- 1 lbs ground beef
- 1 red onion (chopped)
- ½ cup mushroom (sliced)
- 2 cloves garlic (minced)
- 1 cup cabbage (shredded)
- 1 tbsp fish sauce
- 1 tbsp ginger (fresh)
- 1 tbsp apple cider vinegar
- 1 head iceberg lettuce
- 1 tbsp coconut aminos

Garnish:
Shredded cabbage
Chopped onions (green)
Shredded carrot

Directions:

1. In a large skillet, sauté the onions over medium heat and add ground beef to it.
2. Cook the beef for 10-12 minutes, or until the beef is no longer pink in the centre and add ginger and garlic, stirring occasionally, for about 2-3 minutes.
3. Add the cabbage and mushrooms and cook until the vegetables are soft.
4. Pour in vinegar, fish sauce, and coconut aminos while stirring.
5. Remove from the heat and set aside.
6. Wash and dry lettuce leaves and spoon the beef mixture into each leaf, garnishing it with the additional vegetables.

Dinner
Plantain lasagna

(Serves 6)

Ingredients

- 1 can of coconut milk
- 1 large red onion (chopped small)
- 2 medium carrots (chopped small)

- 300g mince beef
- 3-4 garlic cloves (peeled, minced)
- 5-6 large plantains (peeled, cut into thick slices)
- 1 tsp all spice powder
- 1 tbsp olive oil
- Sea salt and black pepper to taste

Directions

1. Preheat your oven to 350 degrees F.
2. In a frying pan over medium heat, add the olive oil and add the plantain and seasonings. Cook them until they are nice and brown on both sides, this should take about 5 to 7 minutes.
3. In another frying pan, cook down the onions and carrots with a little salt, pepper, and all spice powder.
4. Add the beef to it and cook until the beef is browned. Now add the coconut milk to it and let the meat simmer for 15 minutes on low heat.
5. Take a 9x12 inch baking dish and cover with fried plantain below and then about 2 cups of mince beef mixture and cover this with a layer of plantain. Fill the baking dish till the top and bake for 25-30 minutes.

Dessert

(Serves 1)

Chocolatey coffee hazelnut shake

- ½ a banana
- ¼ cup strong coffee
- 1/3 cup hazelnuts
- 1 tsp raw honey
- 1 tbsp cocoa powder
- 1 cup coconut
- A few ice cubes

Directions

1   Blend all of the above ingredients in a blender until well incorporated.

Day 14

Breakfast

Banana avocado morning smoothie

(Serves 1)

Ingredients

- ½ of an avocado
- 1 frozen banana
- ½ a cup unsweetened almond milk
- 1 tbsp nut butter (any)
- 3-4 ice cubes
- Pinch of cinnamon and sea salt

Directions

Blend all the above ingredients in a blender until well incorporated.

Lunch

Salmon Cakes

(Serves 6)

Ingredients:

- 2 eggs
- 2 tbsp onion (chopped)
- 2 cans of pink salmon

- ½ cup almond meal
- ¼ cup parsley (chopped)
- 2 tsp hot sauce
- 1 large sweet potato (cooked and mashed)
- 1 tsp cumin
- 2 tsp paprika
- 2 tbsp coconut oil
- ½ tbsp sea salt
- ½ tsp black pepper
- 1 tbsp fresh lemon juice

Directions:

1. Start by mashing the potato with a fork in a mixing bowl.
2. Now add the lemon juice, almond meal, sea salt, black pepper, cumin, hot sauce, paprika, and parsley to the potato.
3. In another bowl whisk the eggs together and combine it with the mashed potato. Crush the canned salmon using your hands (taking out any skin and bones) and mix it with the potato mixture.
4. Next, using a small measuring cup, scoop out evenly sized cakes. You should make approximately 10-14 patties.
5. Store the patties in the fridge overnight.
6. Heat some coconut oil in a large skillet over medium heat and fry approximately 5-6 patties at a time; cooking them on each side for 4-5 minutes.
7. Serve hot

Dinner

Crockpot chicken stew

(Serves 4-5)

Ingredients:

- 3-4lbs chicken (whole)
- 8 oz mushrooms (chopped)
- 3 carrots (chopped)
- 2 cups cabbage (chopped)
- ¼ bundle spinach
- 2 red onions (chopped)
- 1 large sweet potato (chopped)
- 2 cups stock (chicken)
- 4-5 cloves garlic (peeled, chopped)
- Sea salt and black pepper to taste
- Oregano to taste

Directions:

1. Using a crock pot, put the chicken in the centre. Place all the vegetables around the chicken except for the spinach, and add chicken stock, garlic, and seasonings to your taste.
2. Cover the crock pot and let it cook on low heat for around 8-10 hours and add the spinach 15 minutes before serving.
3. Serve hot.

Dessert

Paleo fruity trifle

(Serves 2)

Ingredients

- 2 ripe peaches (or canned peaches, peeled and cut into slices)
- 5-6 Paleo oatmeal cookies (crushed up)
- 2 cans of coconut milk (chilled)
- ½ tsp vanilla extract
- 1 tbsp grade B maple syrup
- A Handful of sliced almond slivers

Directions

1. Take the cream off of the top of both chilled cans of coconut milk, and add the maple syrup to it, beating with an electric beater until the cream has thickened. Mix in the vanilla extract.
2. Layer the trifle in individual tall glasses, by first carefully placing a few slices of peaches on the bottom and a spoonful or two of the coconut cream, a handful of crushed cookies and then repeat with the peach slices, the coconut cream and cookies until the glass is full.
3. Garnish with some almond slivers before serving.

Chapter 5

Exercise the Paleo way - Get in shape!

Paleo is defined by the balance it requires between what you eat and your daily activity levels. There is no better way to achieve full Paleo benefits then through burning the energy you get from eating high quality, clean, Paleo approved ingredients. The Paleolithic man was as much about activity levels as it was about sustenance and shelter on a daily basis. This prompted natural muscle movement, which we try mimicking through various exercise equipment like weight lifts, elliptical machines and treadmills.

While, there is absolutely nothing wrong with using that equipment to burn Fat and trying to stay fit, the cavemen's fitness was more due to natural activity levels we severely lack today. They were used to walking for lengths of time, looking for food, water and shelter, on rough terrains in unfriendly weather. This served another purpose on a fitness level apart from the obvious need for it. These activities on the whole helped the caveman achieve quicker muscle mass, good reflexes, strengthening of bones and avoid weight problems and other health issues associated with low activity levels today.

a. Low intensity cardio

Low intensity cardio can be in the form of low intensity aerobics exercises, which last 25-30 minutes. This will help in strengthening your abdominal, back, and leg muscles, and tightening your core, giving you a good Fat burn out without the need for rushing to the gym while you're busy, or without the use of any machinery. All you need is a trusted, well known aerobics workout you can learn easily and follow 2-3 times a week.

Apart from low intensity aerobics you can simply opt for low paced walking for 40-45 minutes a day. The walk should not leave you breathless or unable to talk, so think low intensity! Not jogging or running. If you're looking to upgrade your pace, try taking a walk in the wild or go mountain hiking. This sort of low level cardio will help build your strength while working all of your body muscles. Swimming is another low intensity cardio exercise that will strengthen your muscles and help you maintain weight you lose through the diet.

b. Cross fit

Cross fit is a popular combination of exercises which mimic the Paleolithic activity levels and natural muscle movement. This mixes together low intensity workout, lunges, squats, weight lifting, and gymnastics, which together provide a close similarity to the way our ancestors attained their lean and strong bodies. We all know that the cavemen were used to a number of different activities, which constitute as body firming and muscle strengthening or building exercises. This includes, lunging, squatting, sprinting fast once in a while, jumping, climbing, lifting heavy things, throwing weights, dragging or pulling and pushing heavy things. This served as a catalyst in the Stone Ages to increase strength and endurance levels, which if you follow this exercise regime you can achieve as well.

c. Strength and endurance training

Strength and endurance training also resembles movement levels, which are consistent with the caveman's activity levels. Strength –endurance training involves building up muscle mass and being able to maintain that muscle mass after overexerting yourself. This is something athletes are more likely to go for when they're on a Paleo diet because this type of exercise routine helps the athlete use their 'developed' muscles over a longer period of time, and enables them to perform in their chosen field over a longer period of time using varied weight lifting routines to build muscles and increase endurance levels over a period of time.

Simplify your exercise routine. Paleo doesn't have to be a complex lifestyle, you can start slow and build on it. Start with easy exercises you can do at home, lifting heavy things once in a while, walking up and down your stairs, etc. This way you'll get used to activities, which promote natural muscle movement and growth, while burning fats and giving you a leaner physique to look forward to. Just be sure of the goals you're looking to achieve living the Paleo lifestyle because unless you know what you are looking for out of it, you may not understand the results you get from it.

Some tips for Paleo exercise:

- Be sure to stretch before and after your exercise routines. Especially, during exercises like aerobics workouts and weight lifting to avoid incurring injuries.
- For exercises involving performance athletes, make sure you consume a fair amount of Carbohydrates, which will give you the right amount of energy to perform well in your game.
- Don't do too much too soon, start slow and build on them.

Chapter 6

Paleo tips and recommendations for beginners

1.   Be prepared. Make diet charts, meal plans, or keep a food diary. This is the best way to make it easier to transition over to the Paleo lifestyle and give you body time to adjust to the change.

2.   Make sure you fridge is stocked with healthy foods and snacks so that you're prepared to beat a craving; otherwise you'll go back to unhealthy habits.

3.   Read labels of food products for gluten content, sugar, and sodium content. Most commercially processed foods contain gluten (like soya sauce, condiments, bouillon cubes, even some tea). Watch out for sodium content in processed meats, cheese, and canned foods. (canned vegetables are cheaper, but if they have a high sodium and nitrate content, might be best to stick to the fresh variety.)

4.   Cook in bulk. For example, make lots of stock (vegetable/chicken/beef) and freeze the excess

for later use. When you're in hurry you'll be glad you stuffed your freezer with varying degrees of annoyance.

5. Buy most of your vegetables from the farmers market, in their peak season, you'll get them for a good price. Generally, grocery stores charge a higher price as compared to the farmers market.

6. Make a meal out of the weeks leftovers, instead of letting them just go to waste.

7. Try drinking a glass of water before you eat, and always have some vegetables or salads with your main meal to avoid overeating.

8. Take some dietary supplements like Omega 3 oil capsules, anti oxidants, Vitamin D, Calcium (if you're cutting out dairy from your diet), and probiotics because most of the time many of us can't afford grass fed meat, or fresh vegetables; by eating these dietary supplements you can supplement your nutritional levels. But just read the labels first and make sure that all the supplements you choose are free from yeast, gluten, etc.

9. Find some support with friends, a group in your aerobic class, or people on internet forums who are also Paleo followers, so that you can exchange some firsthand tips, and feel comforted that you

have some moral support which helps you and doesn't let you fall back on bad habits.

10. Try eating organ meats by disguising them. For example, if you're using kidney's you can grind it into mincemeat and make chili out of it or tacos. This will make it easier to mentally digest before you can put it in your mouth. Organ meats are the cheapest source of proteins, which are also a powerhouse of nutrients that surpasses normal muscle meat we all buy.

11. Buy a crockpot and learn to cook some tough cuts of meats like ox tail, shanks, trotters, shoulders, etc. These take slow cooking to prepare, but the taste is unbelievably good and also really cheap.

12. Keep caffeine drinking and alcohol at a certain limit like 1-2 coffee cups in a day. See how you're body responds to this. Most of us don't have the luxury to sleep an uninterrupted 7-8 hours every day and need the caffeine.

13. Do a Paleo purge and get rid of all non Paleo ingredients in your fridge and pantry to avoid temptation and make healthier choices.

14. If you visit the farmers market at the end of the day, they will most likely be selling at a cheaper price because they don't want their produce going to waste.

15. Try growing your own fruits and vegetables if you have the space and the can learn how to.

16. Buy some frozen vegetables if you don't have a farmers market near you, or are having a craving for out of season vegetables. Frozen vegetables are available everywhere and are cheaper than buying fresh one sometimes. Just make sure you've enough space in your freezer to accommodate them.

17. If you plan to use legumes, soak them up to 7-8 hours in water and then cook them to drastically lower the phytate and lectin content in them.

18. Find healthier alternatives to gluten based ingredients like coconut flour, almond flours, or even plantain flour. These are a great substitute for the flour we normally use in baking recipes with similar approximately the same ratios.

19. Coconut flour is more drying than other flours and will need more moisture to give good baking results. Try adding fruit puree and more eggs to get a similar texture to baked goods which use wheat flour.

20. If you can't find Paleo ingredients easily in your local stores, try ordering them online. Even Amazon stocks almond flour and coconut flour. There are some online stores which are Paleo

based, so you won't worry about not being able to recreate your favorite desserts.

21. Use sweeteners like palm sugar, agave syrup, grade B maple syrup, and raw honey for desserts in your smoothies and hot drinks. And use coconut aminos instead of soya sauce.

22. Before starting the diet, give you physician a visit and let them do a full health checkup and discuss the changes you'll be making in your diet to them. Especially, if you're suffering from some autoimmune disease or are in any way unwell.

23. Don't start the diet when you're about to shift houses, start your exams, or are starting a new job, or even have a marathon the next week because Paleo requires an adjustment period, which doesn't involve other factors that may interfere with your adjustment to the diet and give some results, which can be attributed to elevated stress levels you're experiencing due to external issues.

24. Try to get at least 7-8 hours of sleep every day. This is an ideal level of sleep that most of us need to thrive on the next day, but make the effort to squeeze in an extra hour by going to sleep an hour earlier than you generally do.

Conclusion

The purpose of this book was to guide Paleo beginners and show them how easy eating and living Paleo can be. Like I said before, there is no pre-arranged formula, which will tell you exactly how much to eat when. Stone Age man was no mathematician or scientist, they didn't rely on macronutrient ratios or had to choose between grain fed meat and the grass fed variety. Paleo as a diet and lifestyle choice is all about following your own Paleo code, which you will be able to form once you've settled into the diet and feel confident enough to take charge of your Paleo journey. This happens only when you've set your goals and know what you need to do in order to achieve those goals. For example, if you want to lose weight using Paleo, you need to map out your daily routine in a food diary, including what you'll eat and your activity levels that should help you lose weight. The best things to do are to listen to your body's response and accordingly make tweaks in the diet to what you eat.

Start by cutting out all the non-approved Paleo ingredients for 30 days at least and see how you feel when you reintroduce some of the grey area foods, which aren't deemed that harmful to human body. This does not include gluten and grains because as an ingredient gluten will always be harmful to the human body in one form or another. But don't fret because Paleo is nothing if not flexible. You can use Paleo substitutes to recreate all those foods you crave and were used to having before you changed over to Paleo. After the initial adjustment period, you'll find yourself more cheerfully accustomed to it because you'll actually start seeing results! This is what eating and living Paleo is all about, getting healthy and maintaining those optimum health levels; don't be unhappy if you fall off the wagon and revert to bad habits, just try and learn from your mistakes and try not to repeat them the next time. Stay Strong!

Good luck for you Paleo beginning!